Koalas

by

Gail Saunders-Smith

Pebble Books

an imprint of Capstone Press

Pebble Books

Pebble Books are published by Capstone Press
818 North Willow Street, Mankato, Minnesota 56001
http://www.capstone-press.com
Copyright © 1998 by Capstone Press
All Rights Reserved • Printed in the United States of America

Library of Congress Cataloging-in-Publication Data
Saunders-Smith, Gail.
    Koalas/by Gail Saunders-Smith.
    p.cm.
    Includes bibliographical references (p. 23) and index.
    Summary: Describes and illustrates various
activities of koalas and their joeys.
    ISBN 1-56065-486-4
    1. Koala--Juvenile literature. 2. Koala--Infancy--Juvenile
literature. [1. Koala. 2. Animals--Infancy.] I. Title.

QL737.M384S38 1997
599.2'5--dc21
                              97-8307
                               CIP
                                AC

Editorial Credits
Lois Wallentine, editor; Timothy Halldin and James Franklin,
design; Michelle L. Norstad, photo research

Photo Credits
Bob Bowdey, cover, 4, 6, 10, 18
Visuals Unlimited/Will Troyer, 8; Carlyn Galati, 3, 12;
    Kjell B. Sandved, 1, 14; Ken Lucas, 16; Cheryl Hogue, 20

Table of Contents

3

A koala
climbs up trees.

A koala eats
eucalyptus leaves.

A koala sleeps on high branches.

10

A koala has
babies.

Babies are
called joeys.

A joey rides
on backs.

A joey learns
to climb up trees.

18

A joey learns
to eat eucalyptus
leaves.

A joey learns
to sleep on high
branches.

Words to Know

branch—a part of a tree that grows out of its trunk like an arm

joey—a young koala

koala—a small, furry animal that lives in trees; it is found in Australia

leaves—the flat and usually green parts of a plant or tree

Read More

George, Linda. *The Koalas of Australia.* Mankato, Minn.: Hilltop Books, 1998.

Powzyk, Joyce. *Wallaby Creek.* New York: Lothrop, Lee and Shepard Books, 1985.

Internet Sites

About Koala—Cuddly, Stubby Little Australian Marsupial Animal
http://ozramp.net.au/~senani/koala.htm

Koala's Page
http://www.geom.umn.edu/~jpeng/KOALA/
    koala.html

Lone Pine Koala Sanctuary — Koala Information
http://www.koala.net:80/animals/koalas.htm

Species Facts: Koala
http://www.lpzoo.com/animals/mammals/
    facts/koala.html

The Australian Koala Page
http://www.aaa.com.au/Koala.html

Note to Parents and Teachers

This book describes and illustrates several behaviors of koalas and their cubs. The clear photographs support the beginning reader in making and maintaining the meaning of the text. The sentence structure provides practice for the child to assume more control of the text. Children may need assistance with the expository vocabulary. Children also may need assistance in using the Table of Contents, Words to Know, Read More, Internet Sites, and Index/Word List sections of the book.

Index/Word List

Word Count: 45